ANTVENTURES
JOURNEY TO PURPOSE

AN ANT'S TALE OF SELF-DISCOVERY

SHARANG ARVIND

BookLeaf Publishing

India | USA | UK

Presentation by *BookLeaf Publishing*

Web: www.bookleafpub.com
E-mail: info@bookleafpub.com

ISBN: 9789367392713

First edition 2025

Dedicated to my father, Dr. Arvind Kumar Srivastava, a renowned surgeon and professor.

For his unwavering dedication to the well-being of everyone around him, especially committing his life to the betterment of the poor.

While you have moved on, you leave behind a legacy of kindness and generosity that continues to inspire me every day.

"People take different roads seeking fulfillment and happiness. Just because they're not on your road doesn't mean they've gotten lost."

— Dalai Lama XIV

CONTENTS

PART 1

A Good Life

Cidaé opened his eyes as the first rays of the sun penetrated the mud hole that was a part of his colony. He marched past the guards and drone ants to the central palace, paid obeisance to his Queen Mother, and turned around, absorbing the beauty around him.

The tunnel with the unborn shells to his left, the food storage area with fresh locust harvest in another corner of the colony, the worker quarters—each part of the Paradise was designed with the best aesthetics in mind. Water seeped through the side of the west wing, joining the puddle that reflected whatever rays of light managed to reach its surface. The air was moist almost all the time, and the breeze was cool. Queen Mother would say that they were born to work for and enjoy the fruits of this beautiful Paradise.

Preparing to start the day's work was never easy for Cidaé, yet he was inspired by the motivating gestures of the guards and the gracefulness with which the workers fell in line. He was a Provider for this Paradise, and he was born on Earth to fulfill this very purpose. Gathering himself, he joined his fellow workers in his troop's line and marched in their steady procession into the routine scuttle of the outside world.

As he exited the Paradise, his eyes were temporarily blinded by the bright sunshine that enveloped everything all around him. They ambled in a single file, looking for clues that would enable them to find enough catch to achieve today's Quota within the next 10 hours. They searched below the dry leaves, over the roots of the trees that jutted out of the earth, around the big rocks, and into the bushes. The September sun was not harsh, but Cidaé dreamt of the Spring when the Outside would be full of colorful flowers and all varieties of insects. In the Spring months, Cidaé could achieve his daily Quota within a couple of hours. Winter was the worst, harsh, unforgiving; almost no food to be found anywhere. Winter was coming.

Kanté, his brother, who also shared his resting quarters back home, nudged him hard. Everyone turned and looked to the right at the same time. Insect movement, a few meters away. They could hear a bzzz bzzz bzzz—the painful call, which meant only one thing. FOOD!

In his childish enthusiasm, Cidaé broke rank and took a few steps towards the target, then froze. He turned around. Dumné, the leader of his brigade, was staring at him with bloodshot eyes. Cidaé retreated in line. This is the third time that Cidaé has dared the insolence of breaking rank, and none other than Queen Mother would have to deal with this. But right now, the pack had to reach the target before any other colonizer got there.

They walked in a single line as fast as they could, their feet marching in unison and with a purpose. Before them lay the biggest beetle that they had ever seen, lying on its back and frantically moving its wings, trying to get back on its feet before any hunter discovered her. There were only eighteen workers in the platoon, and it was almost impossible to take this prize back to the Paradise.

Dumné was quick in giving instructions. Kanté was directed to rush and get backup. The remaining sixteen workers circled the beetle, while Dumné, being the warrior that he was, climbed on her to inspect it. There was no way she could escape. The workers got below it and heaved. Let alone carrying it, they couldn't even move it. Cidaé looked at Dumné in disdain. This was an impossible task, and they had to wait for backup to arrive.

When motivation and threats did not work, Dumné climbed down to help his team. He was their leader after all. With his help, they were able to move the giant beetle but a few centimeters. And then their worst nightmare unraveled.

Bullet ants!

A file of over fifty Bullets was rushing towards them. Now was the time to leave. Cidaé wanted to let go of the beetle and scram, but the only fate that a deserter faces is a painful death at the hands of Queen Mother. The platoon looked at Dumné with hope, anticipating his instruction to leave the prize and escape. Instead, he nodded his head, a silent indication that they have to stand their ground. The workers turned towards the Bullets and prepared for battle. If they die today, the Paradise will give them the highest honor meant for a warrior.

Dumné blocked the first Bullet ant before it got to the prize. With one bite of his fangs, he bit off the head. The next one met the same fate. The workers behind Dumné now stood by his side with pride in their eyes, ready to kill or die.

The onslaught of the Bullet ants overpowered them in no time. Dumné was the first to be torn to shreds. The Bullets knew they had to eliminate the leader first. By the time they got to Cidaé, they could sense both fear and determination in his eyes. One Bullet sliced his leg off with its mandible, and horrible pain overtook him. By the time they were finished, only dying ants and ant parts remained. The Bullets did not bother to finish everyone and rapidly circled the prize.

As they heaved to lift the beetle, the Bullets noticed a dark cloud in the distance, swiftly approaching them. It was Kanté leading an army of hundreds of Paradise workers, all rushing towards them. The decimation was over soon. They took control of the beetle, killed any Bullet that resisted, and picked up their dying workers. Cidaé lay on his back with eyes tight shut, the pain overtaking him as he passed out. A large portion of his left hind leg was missing.

Cidaé woke up in the Paradise next to the puddle. Five other workers had survived, all of them having lost their limbs and eyesight. Dumné and 10 other workers had been martyred. Cidaé was the only survivor who would ever walk again, albeit with a limp.

As Queen Mother lifted her heavy frame, got off the throne, and left her eggs, the colony gasped. This had never happened before. She would be honoring Dumné with the honor of the Warrior, and many generations of ants to come would take inspiration from his sacrifice— laying his life to secure the prize for the Paradise. The Queen Mother lifted her heavy frame, stood on her rear legs, and gently brushed her front legs on Cidaé's head, affection and pride in her eyes. He was the sole survivor to witness this heroism and also fit enough to talk about it. She chose Cidaé to address the Paradise and tell of this glorious tale before her workers left for the next day's work. He would get the next few days off to recover and regain his strength, and his Quota for those days would also be pardoned.

When the usual early morning sunlight penetrated the Paradise, Cidaé was woken up by two Drone guards. They escorted him to the Glory Tower behind the Queen Mother's central palace. The exit hole right above the Tower caught Cidaé's eye. He shrugged off the Drones and limped his way towards the tower, but he did not bow as he passed the Queen.

PART 2

The Escape

Cidaé took his time to walk toward the Glory Tower as thousands of eyes followed him. His limp was unmistakable; his confidence and strut were unbecoming of a worker. Every Drone guard that he passed looked at him with suspicion. He did not have their good physique and build, and a worker walking with his head held high amongst them was making the Drones uncomfortable.

Cidaé turned around and looked at Queen Mother and her eggs one last time. She smiled back at him and nodded encouragingly. Making a role model of a worker every once in a while would give a boost to the colony's morale. Supplies were low and winter was around the corner; she needed all their force to achieve Quotas and keep the colony running.

Once at the base of the tower, Cidaé picked up pace and quickly ascended to the top of the Glory Tower. Locking his gaze with the queen, he started his rehearsed deliverance, exactly as the drones had coached him.

"Dumné was our commander. He died for each one of us and for our Paradise. The prize that he secured will feed our entire colony for one day. His death will remind us every day of the ultimate sacrifice that we as workers make for our colony, our land. His actions will inspire you to go out stronger and achieve more Quota than any worker in the history of our colony."

Thousands around him stood on their hind legs and cheered, but Cidaé was not hearing them. There were a myriad of emotions swirling in his mind. He took three slow, deep breaths, gaze still locked with the queen, and continued.

"Dumné did not deserve to die. He decided to fight the Bullets and secure the prize, knowing fully well that we were heavily outnumbered. His false pride led to the sacrifice of ten of our brothers' lives in addition to his own."

There were gasps all around. The Drones were alert, looking at Queen Mother, waiting for her directions. She kept her stare tightly locked on Cidaé. He continued:

"When your duty overrides your own purpose, you are disillusioned to struggle for survival each day. You march in lines, you toil all day for your Quota, and you collect food for the Storage because you believe it is your duty. The Paradise thrives and flourishes, but do you? Today, I decide to leave this daily grind and set out to discover my true purpose!"

Cidaé bent low on his five functional legs, inhaled, and leaped high to reach the hole above the Tower and squeezed through it. As he emerged on the Outside at the top of the colony, the sound of the commotion below drowned out. Keeping a brisk pace and not turning or looking behind, he kept walking in the direction of the rising sun.

When he stopped next, the sun was shining straight on his back. Cidaé found shelter under a pebble, lay down, and examined his throbbing leg. There was no Quota to achieve today. Nobody was marching behind him to keep pushing him forward. As the realization hit him, he could feel a bolt of energy running from head to toe, the tufts of hair on his back and sides stretching like pins. He was free to do what he had always tried to do while parading in his ant lines, for which he had been chided time and again. Explore at will!

For three days, Cidaé walked towards the Sun. He would enjoy the warmth when he wanted to, or lie back and look at the blades of grass swaying in the gentle breeze. Instead of feeling stuck with the Quota weighing him down, he felt stronger every day. Finding food for himself was a piece of cake, compared to working all day gathering food for the Storage at the Paradise. As night fell, he would take shelter under a rock and look at the infinite stars in the sky until sleep overtook him.

On the fourth day, Cidaé woke up to a cuckoo bird's call. The pain in his injured leg was dwindling, and a stub was forming at the end of it. Between the bird's calls, Cidaé could hear the burbling sound of water flowing in the distance. How had he missed this sound through the night? Curiosity took over him, and he started walking in the direction of the water. For one hour he walked, the sound getting louder with every step. Cidaé climbed over a rock and looked around. It was clear water flowing in a stream, pebbles lined across its bed, dragonflies hovering in a dance all around its banks. Cidaé's eyes followed the source of the water and saw the dark shadow of deep green woods in the distance, the stream slithering out of it as a snake emerges from its hole. The air was fresh and pleasant to breathe, not musty like the Paradise. The beauty of his surroundings engulfed him, crashing against his senses, painting vivid images of what boundless freedom truly felt like to his imagination.

Following the edge of the stream, Cidaé walked on the half-moist earth, determined to reach the magical woods. His tube-shaped heart was full of desire, the fall season feeling like spring. So when he noticed her light brown back and an electric jolt coursed through him, sending a sharp, unexpected twitch rippling down his side, he desperately attributed it to the enchanting ambiance surrounding him. But deep down, he knew it was her captivating presence that made him acutely aware of his own self, stirring a newfound consciousness within him.

She almost read him from the distance and smiled. And then this stranger started approaching him! Who was this creature in this magical land? Was this some queen whose colony had been attacked and destroyed?

She came close to his face, adjusting the soft tufts of hair on her sides with those slender legs. Her body size matched his, her light brown eyes penetrating his own dark eyes. Cidaé backed down and crouched, unsure whether this was a hunt and he would soon be surrounded by other workers of her colony. She stretched her front legs and brushed them against his. It was a friendly move. Cidaé bumped his mandible against hers, sealing the bond.

Nimmé introduced Cidaé to the free world. Auroria was a society with justice, free will, and equality at the heart of all decision-making within their colony. They gave equal rights to all ants and an equitable distribution of work. Their Queen had dedicated her life to the service of all members of the community. Marching in line was only during the hunting hours. The ants were encouraged to wander for 2 hours each day for self-discovery. Fitness sessions and community feasting ensured the well-being of every member. The forest provided suitable resources for them to thrive.

Cidaé looked down at his stub. He recalled the searing pain and the fear he had experienced in the Bullet attack. All of what Nimmé was telling him seemed unreal. These were foreign civilizations not very far away from the Paradise, more advanced than them yet considerate of each colony member's individuality. Yes, rules were created for the colony to function, but they were relaxed enough to allow self-discovery and happiness. For the Paradise, happiness was in the selfless service of the colony, while in Auroria, happiness lay outside of their work hours.

Cidaé was skeptical to accept Nimmé's invitation to visit her colony. If any foreigner walked into his own Paradise, they would be hunted down and devoured in no time. Curiosity got the better of him, and he walked into Nimmé's lands alongside her. The inside was as magnificent as his Paradise, green moss covering the grounds wherever sunlight broke through the top, interspersed with tiny blue flowers that produced sweet nectar. There was no mandate to walk in lines inside the colony. Group events were a daily affair, and caring for their health and well-being was as important as caring for their colony. Cidaé was amused to see ants huddling together, stretching their bodies in synchrony, experimenting with breathing techniques, and stretched body positions. Nimmé's Queen welcomed Cidaé with a grand ceremony, honoring his resolve and courage to leave his past life and join them in their blessed lands. They were extremely curious to know the ways of the Paradise, and for two days Cidaé obliged them with minute details of his lands. Hearing his tale of their daily struggle for survival, Nimmé's Queen did not hide her pride. She was the founder of this advanced society, starkly superior to the other menial ant colonies that they knew of.

Cidaé was impressed with this society and the freedom that came with it. Their lives had more meaning than just serving their colony. The two hours of exploration were his favorite activity during the entire day. In the coming days, he was assigned a Quota, but he had comfort and safety in these lands, and he was close to his Nimmé; what more could he ask for?

As time passed and the initial excitement of becoming an immigrant citizen of this colony was over, Cidaé's restlessness returned. He felt a sense of déjà vu as he realized he did not belong here, and this was not why he had left the Paradise. He ached to explore other lands. Having discovered Auroria, the prospect of finding even more exciting places triggered him now more than ever.

He gathered the courage to approach his new Queen and confess this to her, confident that she would understand him and offer some advice. The Queen was not surprised or taken aback. Clearly and confidently, she explained the dangers of the world and the safety and freedom that her colony had to offer. Any individual would give up their past lives to be a part of this beautiful society. He would be a fool to venture out when everything he could ever dream of was already there.

Cidaé did not sleep the night. He knew he would regret it deeply, but before dawn broke, he left his Nimmé and his new home and escaped again.

PART 3

The Encounters

As Cidaé moved through the clearing, his shoulders drooped and his abdomen dragged on the ground. For the first time since leaving the Paradise, he felt defeated. He could not believe he had done it again. What was he looking for? Even Nimmé's land could not provide him any sense of stability. He had always felt he was special, but today he was almost ready to consider that he was nothing but a lunatic, an indecisive, disoriented individual who would not fit into the norms of any society. He will die alone without any companion by his side; his body will rot in an unknown cave, and his soul will be trapped under some stone for eternity.

Cidaé took a deliberate pause. He had to get his act together and pull his own weight. Like a child sorting and picking his favorite ingredient out of his bowl, Cidaé tried to disentangle and arrange his thoughts one by one. In the hope of getting divine intervention, he turned his head to look at the Sun when his eyes fell on a hill close by. Dragonflies were hovering over it like drunk dancers around a bonfire. It seemed to call out to him, wooing him with promises of discovery, beckoning him to leave behind the familiar and venture into the unknown. Cidaé decided to climb the hill.

Up close, Cidaé could see the peculiar round shape of the rock, which seemed to rise and fall like a life form breathing in its sleep. Crawling to the top of the rock, Cidaé looked down at two tunnels going down from the sides into the rock, with gigantic flaps manning the entrance. He cautiously crawled toward one of the holes when the rock shook violently and rose into the sky. Terrified, Cidaé scrambled to the edge of the tunnel, biting its mandible deep into the skin to hold on. The trumpeting sound that followed would resonate in Cidaé's head for the rest of his life.

The power and majesty of this creature were indescribable. Cidaé sat at the edge of the ears of the giant, sometimes sinking its mandible deep and holding tight until the giant shook its head violently. Could he make the giant dance to

his wishes? Cidaé tunneled deep inside the ear to see what he was capable of. The more Cidaé tunneled, the more the creature trumpeted in pain. Finally, he crawled out of the ear and onto the temple of the giant. Looking all around, he could see the endless horizon and feel the majesty of this beast. Was freedom all about having absolute power, the ability to command unmatched strength to bend any creature at your will? How was it then that this beast had been vanquished by his own tiny, minuscule self!

Did Queen Mother back in the Paradise feel the same power? She was free after all, commanding thousands of ants like him. They would kill and die for her any day. Cidaé had a sudden urge to head back to the Paradise and tell everyone about this sublime beast. They will see the futility of their mundane daily existence, abandon the Paradise, and instead go with him to experience the unexplored world, its majestic creatures, and its mysteries.

Cidaé leaped off the beast and landed softly on the grass. He crawled at a slow pace, brooding about heading back to the Paradise. His broken stub had now healed, but it would never support his body weight again. Involved in his thoughts, he stopped near a bush, looking up at the light blue sky. The leaves on the bush blocked the sun in patches, making an intricate pattern on the ground. As he sat observing the mesh of light earth and dark shadow, it shook gently. His ant senses knew this could mean only one thing. Predator!

Turning back, Cidaé saw a dark yellow chameleon crawling on the bush, its head pointed straight at him. Cidaé scampered away from the bush as fast as he could when he heard the whiplash of the predator's tongue landing right next to him. He could see death closing in on him. Cidaé froze, too scared to move, eyes closed, waiting for the next attempt to get pulled into the mighty jaws and feel his body parts get crushed into a black mass of pulp. Nimmé, Queen Mother, and Dumné's faces flashed before his closed eyes.

A few silent moments passed. Wondering why he wasn't dead yet, Cidaé opened his eyes slowly, turned around, and saw the chameleon frozen, its mouth open, tongue and jaws still aimed at him. Yet its eyes were looking away from him. Cidaé followed the gaze of the predator and noticed a bright yellow snake, like a sculpture set in stone if not for the flickering tongue, waiting to pounce on the chameleon and swallow it whole.

The unusual threesome, without movement, frozen in time.

PART 4

Enlightenment

The essence of life that he had been searching for dawned upon him like the floodlights illuminating a stadium at night. Cidaé started running in the direction of the Paradise, tumbling many times yet full of zealous hope about the message that he was carrying for his colony. Barely resting, it took him 2 full days and nights to reach the entrance of his homeland. The morning workers were just leaving for duty, and Cidaé slipped in through one of the less-used openings. Before the Drone guards could realize it was him, he had entered the Queen's chambers. Mother stared at her prodigal son, shocked to the core, unable to react. The Drones lined up behind him, ready to slice him to pieces at one gesture of the Queen Mother. Yet she allowed him to speak, and Cidaé blurted out about his adventures: the lonely trail, the alluring stream,

Nimmé's world and her rights and freedom, the majestic beast that could be controlled by his tiny self, and his miraculous escape from death.

Facing death in the face made him realize that the Earth has much more to offer than survival for the basics. Every life form on Earth had beaten billions of odds against itself just to be here. The miracle of birth bestowed upon each living being was meant for discovery, exploration, and finding true happiness within the means of each one of us. He was here to take Queen Mother and the colony with him and discover true happiness with his own people. His encounters had proven that there was so much to discover, so much to experience. They were locked in a small enclosure, beautifying its chambers in the hopes of building a better colony for a brighter future, while the real world outside was already perfectly crafted for them in the present day. Surely there had to be some other place away from the Paradise that would provide for each of them in abundance, make them realize their full potential, and bring more wisdom and fulfillment to every member of the colony.

The Queen had never been stubborn; she did not have an ego like her own mother. She had given more freedom to her children and had heard her subjects more than any generation before her. She recalled how, as a child, she had seen real slavery. In those days, not meeting the Quota meant torture or even death. She had left those cursed lands to build a colony with better rights for all. And this is why it was only herself to blame that one of her own children had strayed, disregarding the good life she had given him, and was now living in a world of fantasy, devoid of reality, dreaming of non-existent mystical lands.

She looked down upon him with disdain, then asked with a straight expressionless face.

"Would self-discovery feed the colony and all of our babies? Without the Quota, when our Paradise starves, who will stop the ants from cannibalizing each other; who will control the anarchy? You waltz into my Paradise that gave you food and protection and rights, and you audaciously suggest that I abandon my own land and follow you in search of fantasy, not even knowing where to go? You are my blood; I have allowed you to disrespect me twice. But you will not die today. You will be a living example of failure and underachievement. Every descendant born in this colony will know the story of Cidaé the betrayer and deserter, who brought disgrace to the esteemed duties of the worker ant and who will eventually die anonymous and alone, with no achievements to his name except to bring shame to our Paradise. You will now walk out and never come back!"

Hundreds of eyes followed the lone creature as he crawled across the floor, half dragging himself, leaving a trail of disgrace. He looked steadily down, avoiding eye contact with his brothers, workers who had poured back in droves to watch him confront Queen Mother.

Loneliness is a curse. Social animals cannot survive without the bond, stimulation, and sense of growth and achievement that they get in their societal existence. Standing out in the crowd, realizing you are lonely, different, and incompetent is an imprecation, and Cidaé felt it through the core. He wished Queen Mother had ordered the drones to finish him off—a painless death without resulting in this humiliation.

So when Kanté blocked Cidaé's march of disgrace, gently tapping his mandible to indicate solidarity, a renewed lease of life and hope rushed through his body. For the first time since he had entered the Paradise, he paused to look all around at the eyes staring at him before stopping at Kanté, his Brother and once again his savior after the Bullet attack. They say a blade of grass is enough to save

a drowning ant. With his shoulders lifted, his head held up high, his gait almost transforming like a shape-shifting wizard, without even glancing at the Queen, Cidaé shouted aloud, "My Brothers, come explore the world with me, or die with the regret of being an inconsequential number who built this Queendom." The two Brothers, who had never shared any bond before except loyalty to the Paradise and the Queen, walked side by side, slowly and elegantly, nonchalant about the whispers and murmurs behind them.

Once outside their nest, the social obligations binding Cidaé and Kanté vanished into thin air. Like prisoners getting early parole, only in this case, the parole was for breaking rules and bad behavior. Behind them, ten other Brothers followed suit. Each inhabitant of the Paradise knew deep down that something was wrong in their lives, but only these twelve dared to break their shackles and walk out. Every one of the twelve Brothers knew they were walking into nothingness, possibly failure, maybe death, but their spirits were to be their guide. And of course, they trusted Cidaé to know where to go. He did!

For three days, the twelve walked side by side, without syncrony. At first, it was difficult to walk out of order; they would inadvertently start marching in a line, then realize their renewed lives and once again embrace the lawlessness in their amble. The Paradise did not guard them, but they felt secure with their Brothers beside them.

The stream was as mesmerizing as Cidaé had experienced it the first time. The Brothers sat beside the flowing water, admiring the scenery for many hours. However, Cidaé had more to do. He could not go on this quest without his friend.

Surely Nimmé will agree to go with him.

He knew exactly where she would be in her self-discovery hours. As he had expected, he found her at the edge of the forest, leaning on a stone, diligently observing the patterns of the intricate leaves on the trees that made up the forest. Cidaé knew how much she enjoyed comparing different forms and geometries in nature, which he found both annoying and infatuating at the same time. Why did she always invoke these opposing emotions in him, he wondered.

But of course, she heard him! Most of their communication had been without words. They locked their gaze, their hearts smiling within, although their faces were without expression, delaying the gratification that would come from rushing toward each other.

PART 5

The Enchanted Lands

Cidaé was not alone when he marched into Auroria. He held Nimmé's arm as his Brothers spoke confidently of their quest, with a firm belief that this advanced civilization would understand them. Nimmé's Queen was not happy with the entry of these foreigners, but her own rules allowed any differing and counter opinions to be heard. She warned her subjects not to leave their free land and venture into danger and death. And they complied, all except five of her children, five brave who were not looking for a secure and comfortable life but for the pursuit of adventure.

And so this motley of eighteen set off in their search of the unknown. Despite the hesitation of his newfound family, Cidaé decided not to circle the woods and walked

32

straight into them. Legends in both their cultures had warned them of the dark tales of the forest, the fire-breathing specters, and cannibal tribes. Daylight deluded the forest, and strange sounds would echo through the cold, wet nights; spirits would devour anyone daring to venture into their lands. Cidaé had been practical. He had always questioned the laid-down rules, the stories of faith, and of higher powers and demons, albeit in his head. Now he had the freedom to speak up and exchange his views with his tribe.

The forest was dark other than small beams of sunlight in patches that could penetrate the thick cover of leaves. Sinté from Nimmé's lands was the sharpest of them all. She had a knack of smelling out danger, and Cidaé had learned to trust her instincts early on. Within the precincts of the forest, Sinté spontaneously took the lead, and the rest followed on. To their amazement, the deeper they walked into the forest, the less dense it became until it was bright as day with just a flimsy coverage of trees. The foliage changed, bright yellow and red flowers popping all around them, a colorful warning of the adventures ahead of them.

Far up ahead, Sinté spotted a clearing where the bright afternoon sun shone brightly. It felt like a calling, and they walked for an hour before they reached the open space. It was a huge, shallow crater, covered with light green grass all across and a single large, dazzling blue rock in the middle of the depression. The Sun's rays reflected from the rock as well as the grass, making the entire clearing shine bright in the middle of the forest. Despite Sinté's inhibitions, the site was impossible to resist for them. Eventually, each member of this tribe started walking towards the middle of the clearing, as if mesmerized. Cidaé noticed that every tuft of grass in the crater bent towards the rock as if paying homage to a deity. At the tip of each grass was a tiny crystal hanging from the top of the blade, and the reflection from thousands of these crystals was what was making the crater glitter with myriad colors in the sunlight. As they walked towards the center, they could notice the crystals grow in size, making the grass blades bend a little more and the center of the clearing even brighter.

Kanté was the first to taste a piece of crystal. His eyes numb with disbelief, he plucked the crystal with his mandible, swallowing it whole. It was the sweetest element his mouth had ever experienced, a hundred times sweeter than the nectar that he had tasted from the flowers back in the Paradise. Unable to stop himself, he stretched to pluck another one. Before he could reach it, the grass around

him transformed into an intense fluorescent green. The blue rock in front of him seemed to throb as if alive. Kanté stared in front of him, bewitched by the Queen Mother's gigantic figure, sparkling blue and a thousand times larger, emerging from under the grass in front of him. This was a strange, unknown feeling of freedom. He was not scared; he was happily admiring the colors that were weaving in front of his eyes. Turning his head to look back at the forest, he could see purple vines circling the barks of the trees; the leaves themselves transformed into vivid shapes, round and square and prism.

Sinté was the last to taste the crystal. Before eating it whole, she looked around at her tribe, eyes lost, lying on their backs, a peculiar smile on their faces. This had to be the awakening that they wanted to experience and had left their homes for! As she crushed the crystal under her mandible, she could feel the sweet energy hit her body, the world transforming in front of her into alternating colors, vivid patterns, and contrasting exposures.

Cidaé did not realize how long he had slept. When he opened his eyes, a deep blue hue lit everything up around him. It was the moon's light illuminating the dark sky, intensified by the blue energy of the rock. Unlike the forest, the crater had no sounds, no rustling of leaves, no cicadas chirping abuses at each other. Cidaé felt for any vibrations under his feet. Nothing. Looking around, he found Nimmé on her back, still under the spell of the crystals. Limping towards her, he lay down against her abdomen, hoping to live the moment with his beloved while absorbing the beauty around him.

The sound of dripping water broke his trance. It was trickling from the edge of the crater like a waterfall, slowly collecting in the middle around the base of the rock. Cidaé was struck with fear, like a gazelle in the line of sight of a leopard. He had to get out of the crater now, but his tribe was incapacitated. He shook Nimmé hard with his mandible, rocking her body back and forth, then bit her hard near the neck. Wincing, she woke up. Before she could react, a strong gush of water displaced them both, pushing them closer to the rock. Cidaé's eyes burned with the water. Nimmé coughed up the salt water she had swallowed. The tribe was off the spell now, panicking, vomiting the concentrated salt water, and holding on to the blades of grass as water rushed around their legs. Cidaé had to act now. He was responsible for ensuring the survival of his tribe, but he would not be foolish like Dumné. He had to think on his feet to be able to tide this and save them all. The edge of the crater was far away; they would never make it out in time. The center of the crater was filling fast; water was already at the base of the rock like a moat around a castle. Pointing towards it, Cidaé led the way as they rushed towards the rock, slipping and choking on the water. Closer to the edge of the rock, they realized the moat was too deep and the rock too far out of reach. Turning back was futile. With death inevitable, Cidaé glanced at Sinté for any help.

Sinté grabbed Cidaé's leg with her jaws, gesturing at them to form a chain. Holding on tightly to each other, they jumped into the moat full of water with all their might. The water was rushing in with full force now, making them go in swirls around the blue rock like a whirlpool. Kanté, who was manning the back of the chain, was bumped against the rock and pulled himself with all his might. The chain of eighteen ants hit the rock together, just in time to crawl out of the water and onto the rock. Their eyes and throats burned, but there was no time. The water level was rising, and they had to move to the top of the rock. Letting go of each other, they raced to the top as the water filled the crater and chased them over the blue rock. At the top, the tribe huddled together, the water now covering most of the rock, a sinking island that would take them beneath with itself.

And then, like magic, the gushing water stopped. The tribe cowered close to each other, surrounded by this lake of seawater in the middle of the forest. Their stomachs hurt with the salt water they had swallowed. The tiny hair on their abdomen had been singed. It then dawned upon Cidaé that the forest was testing their will and ability to survive together.

The first rays of morning lit up the rock, the warmth penetrating their exterior to soothe the soul. The rock was as cold as ever, daring the Sun to try harder. They noticed the water starting to recede and disappear under the rock. The grass slowly emerged from under the water, the sweet crystals starting to form again at their tips, waiting to entice the next life that dared enter its realm.

The tribe slid off the rock, moving silently under the grass, looking down to avoid any temptation of the crystals. Emerging from the crater, they looked back only once at this mysterious place before moving on, now huddled closer to each other.

They moved deeper into the forest, never questioning Cidaé on his decisions. He had managed to lead this disparate group of individuals into and out of danger without ever using threat or humiliation. Trusting him had become the norm for them; mutual respect and love for each other made up the pillars of this tribe. He now understood how futile it was for any colony to create set rules and use consequences to enforce those meaningless rules.

Nine days they walked into the forest, the covering so thick that it was impossible to distinguish day from night. A swarm of yellow fireflies was traveling slowly in one direction as if leading the way. The group would follow the swarm until it would suddenly gather pace and disappear ahead. The next day, they were led by a swarm of blue fireflies, and then teal and pink and white. The forest became more and more colorful each day, nature's palette treating their eyes as they marched along. Leaves the color of emerald, ruby, and sapphire shook with each gust of wind. Flowers of every shape and size burst in a riot of colors, their petals with unseen fades, their perfume an addiction that hit all their senses. The creatures they saw, the sounds they heard, and the experiences they had would remain with them for the remainder of their lives. It was empowering to know that they had endured these experiences and survived, yet humbling to realize the vastness of this universe that they had discovered.

Several days passed before they realized they had been ascending. The climb was now steep, but the foliage remained. When they would find an open spot where the

sunlight hit the Earth, they would stay for hours gazing at the majestic hill that materialized in front of them. It would be many more days of tireless ascent before they reached the top of the mountain, a flat landmass high above the horizon.

Kanté's curiosity confronted him once again when he spotted the tiny mushroom. It was the size of his leg, white with red polka dots on the umbrella. Having learned his lesson with the crystals, he neatly avoided going anywhere near this bewitching fungus. As they moved on, the mushrooms grew in size and number, until they were surrounded by a colony of thousands of such fungi, from as gigantic as their Paradise to as small as sand grains, like patterns on a bedsheet spread out over the entirety of the hill. Towering trees with bright lilac flowers interspersed the sea of mushrooms, their barks covered in tree sap that brought a golden hue to the otherwise red-and-white landscape of the fungi. Thick green vines fell from the trees onto the ground, creating a landscape that was rich in fauna and thriving with life.

PART 6

The Civilization

Cidaé's universe was a visual delight, but to the tribe, it was the emotional validation of arriving home. There was always an excitement of discovering something new. The sap secreted from the barks of the towering trees was sweet as manna, tingling their senses when they thrust their mandibles into it, then dissolving into their bodies, releasing its warmth from the insides. They would eventually discover that these lands were like one colossal organism, interconnected and communicating through the fungi and the sap from the trees.

The tribe soon became a part of the ecosystem. They would sit in a ceremonious circle, creating musical notes using their feet, devour any dying fauna, drink the manna from the trees, or find edible fungi that unraveled

their senses and revealed more about the philosophical questions on life and the universe. Nimmé discovered a colony of aphids that would secrete nectar when she rubbed on their bellies; consuming it would open new horizons in their minds. With stimulants that challenged their beliefs, the tribe would sit and brood on their reality for hours together. Their unique diet was just a medium to help them deliberate clearly on their purpose of becoming a part of these Enchanted Lands.

The culture of discovering and deliberating freely with a strong sense of purpose became the hallmark of the tribe. Over time, they established a village that would flourish for generations to come. They built their houses from the umbrellas of the mushrooms, reared aphid farms under the vines, and cared for them like their own. Cidaé recognized the power of emptying his mind of all thought and focusing on only one mental picture for long periods of time. It was a difficult technique to master, but once the tribe got a hang of it, they did not stop at dissecting any problem. Because there were no inhibitions and each one of them was aligned with the one goal of uncovering newer mysteries, the tribe evolved into an advanced civilization in no time.

Cidaé often thought of another multiverse where he was still in the so-called Paradise, toiling to ensure the survival of his colony, constricted in imagination and restricted in action. Every day would be spent toiling with the modest reward of going back to his hole for rest, and every night would be spent loathing the Quota for the next day, in a never-ending cycle of dread. Even with all her resources at her disposal, Queen Mother could never have found what he had started because she was busy propagating the myopic values passed down to her instead of opening up to the possibilities of the future. It pained him to imagine the degradation of his Brothers in those forsaken lands ironically referred to as Paradise, yet it was moot to lead them to civilization because they were slaves of tradition, not creation.

The tribe rapidly multiplied to hundreds of free souls, each generation carrying the legacy of asking questions, challenging established norms, and living in sustenance with their surroundings. Cidaé and Nimmé cared for every member like their own child. As a morning ritual, Cidaé would limp to the largest mushroom, meditating near its stalk until his tribe joined him. He would then throw any question that gatecrashed his mind at them, and the tribe would discuss the possible solutions and what they would tackle that day. They would then scuttle around arranging the tools for that activity, much like inquisitive children during a treasure hunt, the frenzy to create something new consuming them.

One day, when Cidaé did not turn up for meditation, the tribe realized that he had passed away peacefully in his sleep. They did not mourn his death; they celebrated his life, his teachings, and his discoveries. They told the young ones the tales of the journey that he led and the encounters he had to survive to reach this place and build the Village. They did not bury him; instead, they placed his body on the tree bark to be covered in translucent golden sap forever, a perpetual inspiration for every tribe member who came after them. His missing leg reminded them of not venturing into foolishness and chaos, his form reminding them of the blessed life they led at the Village every day.

For one hundred years the civilization prospered, every generation building on the foundations laid by their ancestors, challenging norms and rules, eliminating basic struggle altogether. The Village evolved into a society where nothing was constant, continuous change the only law, debate the only method to address conflict. The one static was Cidaé's body, preserved as a memorial of unflinching respect for the founder of their Society.

PART 7

Timur

Timur was lucky to be born in the Village. He was smaller than his peers, a portion of his left hind leg missing ever since he stumbled out of his shell. In any other colony, he would not have survived, but in the Village, he was cared for. He grew up watching the ants around him living a carefree life, a perennial cloud of contentedness enveloping them. The tribe thrived on extracting the most out of their time on earth, experimenting, debating, building stuff, and trying the edibles this land had to offer.

In his early days, Timur tried mingling with his peers, learning about every tiny detail in the magical Village and the fungi, even participating in the constructive debates that challenged their thoughts. He was the sharpest of them all, yet there was a persistent dissatisfaction in his tiny head. As he grew, Timur's dissatisfaction turned to frustration and eventually to loathing. He started detesting the ways of the tribe, especially the edibles that incapacitated them and made them weak. He would feel the bile rise to his mouth seeing his tribe taking their current situation for granted, considering themselves above other ants because they had been born in luxury, devoid of realistic, hard-working lives that ants were born to lead. They never hunted together as brothers or brought glory to their tribe. How peculiar and unnatural of females to walk around debating and building instead of caring for and rearing their eggs. For nights together, he would lay awake looking at the moon, brooding about the decay that this tribe had brought upon itself. Surely, this was not what Cidaé had wanted to build!

When he finally opened up about his beliefs, the tribe encouraged him to debate about those with them. They knew that with the right reasoning, Timur being the smartest of them all would see the logic of sustaining the Village through discovery, debate, and democracy. Instead, he would insist on his radical views of bringing machoism and discipline to the Village. This is when they started avoiding him, which made him seethe further with exasperation and hate, like acid devouring the wings of a fly.

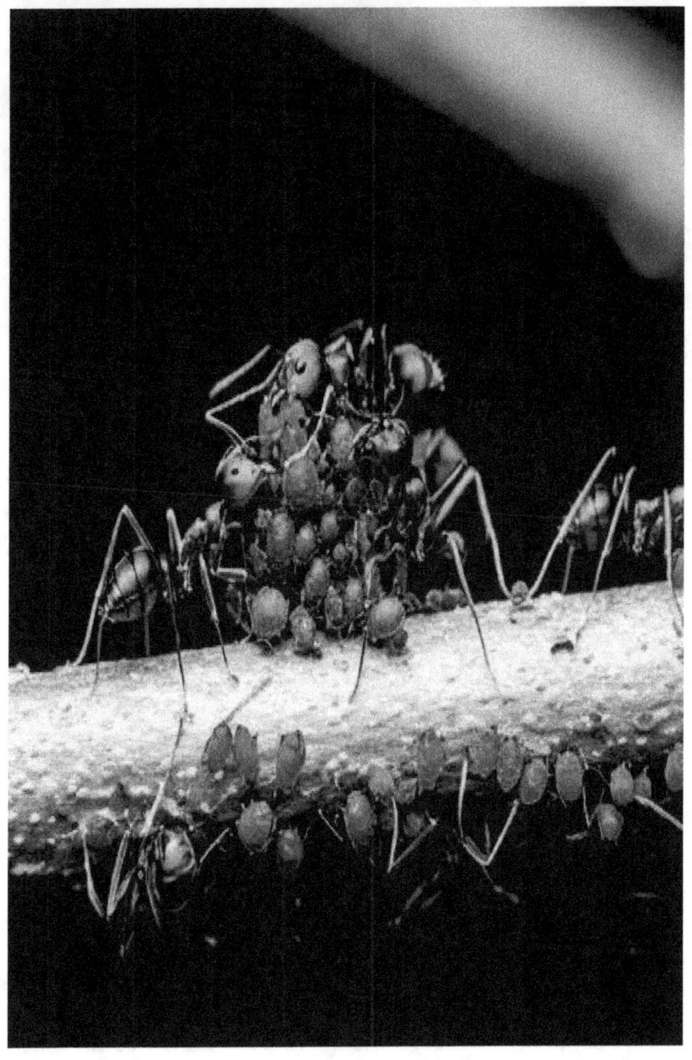

The tribe's worries started when Timur began to attract a fan following, especially among young adults. Though small in number, they were mostly huddled together most of the time. They would boycott the daily debate rituals and refuse to eat the sap from the trees or the secretions from the aphids. On some days, this obsessive group would limp all day to honor Timur and Cidaé's missing leg, drawing comparisons between them. Gradually and steadily, Timur emerged as a cult leader with a fanatical following, a group that would openly challenge the Village's customs and even the purpose of the tribe. All of this was new for the elders; they were not prepared for what was coming at them next.

The aphids were their first target. Timur's group entered the aphid nursery and culled each one of them, adults and infants, eradicating the supply of nectar altogether. The majority of the tribe watched them, a new feeling of fear engulfing them. Some even reasoned that it could be the right thing to do; Timur was trying to help the tribe. The tribe's inaction gave newfound confidence to him, and from that moment on, Timur was unstoppable. He called all the ants and spoke of the degradation of their society and the need to preserve traditions. He talked about preparing the wise to be the hammer and not the anvil, to enforce the Ant laws, because if the tribe wishes to live and move forward, they are forced to eliminate others who come in the way of their colony's survival. Nothing is possible except anarchy unless one's will commands and is obeyed by others, beginning at the top and ending at the very bottom. This is the only way that the coming generations will be looking back with pride, heads held high, that the legacy of Cidaé continues and is not lost in depravity.

Timur's group, now his army, believed every word he uttered. Some would injure a portion of their left hind leg as a mark of respect to him. Most of them believed him to be their savior from the clutches of modern corruption. The frenzy of bringing order and law back to the tribe consumed each one in the army.

Of course, everyone in the Village was petrified to speak up or oppose the army; the majority was not comfortable, but they bore it as a phase that would pass and sanity would eventually prevail. Some of the elders who could see the ensuing destruction of their freedom and civilization and decided to speak up were quickly eliminated. It initially started in the dead of night, then during the daytime, and finally in public executions as the crowd cheered on.

Timur's army banned the rearing of aphids and limited the quantity of tree sap consumption. The mushrooms were declared sacred, and their consumption was prohibited. He divided the ants into classes based on the work that they would do. Policing was the most honorable of all the jobs, reporting directly to the army. The builders came next, responsible for building hills for the colony's expansion and pulling down the Village houses made by their ancestors. Then came the hunters, who would have the honor of hunting and bringing food to the colony. And finally, the female rearers, who would stay within the safety of the hill and care for the eggs and the babies. This division brought efficiency and helped the colony expand rapidly. The ant hills were built upwards to one day become as tall as the trees. Open debates and discussions were forbidden, and free thinking was declared an act of treason.

Timur's reign saw the establishment of his cult, which turned into a movement as his colony flourished. Cidaé was declared the Lord of all ants in the universe, and Timur as his messenger. Statues of Cidaé and Timur were created by the builders and set up at prominent places across the lands.

Through all of this, Cidaé's soul looked on from under the tree sap. He would have to wait for many generations before another insignificant ant dared to challenge the rules and set out to find its purpose, helping restore the civilization to its original glory. And then this cycle of Enlightenment and Darkness would carry on, enduring until the very end of Earth.

Epilogue

"Hope is a good thing, maybe the best of things, and no good thing ever dies."

Many generations after Timur's reign of tyranny, the memory of Cidaé's Village still lingered on in the whispers and the stories passed down among the ants. The ideas of free will and open debate were never fully extinguished, even in the darkest of times. Policing was rampant and unforgiving, and the majority conformed, but there were many silent souls who did not believe Timur's narrative of glory and sought a better life for themselves.

The ant hills were now reaching higher than the trees and teeming with life, with hundreds of thousands of builders, hunters, and rearers making up the majority of the inhabitants. One such inhabitant was Young Myra, a rearer who lived deep inside the ant hills and took care of the eggs and the babies. Like all rearers, she was restricted from venturing outside the colony. Little did her sisters know that she would break tradition and sneak out every night, exploring the forest and the mushrooms, surveying Cidaé's mummified form, gazing at the stars, and reflecting on her life's purpose!

One night, while wandering under the trees not far from her hill, Myra stumbled upon an ancient carving jutting out from between the roots of a great tree, hidden in plain sight. All night, Myra dug through the earth around the carving, eventually discovering the remains of one of the houses razed down many generations ago by Timur's army. It narrated the story of Cidaé's village—a place of exploration, critical thinking, and freedom. Captivated by her discovery, Myra felt a stirring in her heart. She found her purpose at that moment—to revive this forgotten legacy and restore Cidaé's society.

Myra started by sharing her discovery with others, encouraging them to visit the Village House themselves and witness its existence firsthand. Before the police were aware of the existence of the ruins and could raze them down, hundreds of ants had already seen this mystical place. They now knew that Cidaé was not the Lord of the universe but a regular ant like them, an adventurer who wanted to explore the world and build a better life for himself and his tribe. Together, they reignited the spirit of the Village, with conversations of revolt against Timur's army rampant in alleyway chatter inside the ant hills. As Myra's community grew, the hollowness of Timur's oppressive system lay exposed, eventually crumbling like a castle built of a pack of cards.

Their resentment against the rigid administration reached its pinnacle until one day Myra, accompanied by thousands of her followers, stopped working for the regime and staged a walkout. The outnumbered Timur's army watched helplessly as Myra's tribe laid the foundations to build a new Village next to the ant hills. The work was difficult, and they struggled with direction, but the belief in a better future kept them strong. Inspired by Cidaé's legacy and Myra's determination, the ants rose together to reclaim their freedom and dismantle the remnants of Timur's myopic regime.

The Village, now restored to its original glory, flourished under Myra's leadership. It became a living tribute to the movement started by Cidaé, shunning irrational tradition and embracing a spiritual awakening. Cidaé's spirit lives on not in the Village alone but in the hearts of every individual who believes in a world where exploration, courage, and insatiable curiosity thrive.